D0209592

To: Aiden

From:

Sheridan

Illustrated by Martha Day Zschock
Designed by Heather Zschock

Copyright © 2011
Peter Pauper Press, Inc.
202 Mamaroneck Avenue
White Plains, NY 10601
All rights reserved
ISBN 978-1-4413-0648-7
Printed in China
7 6 5 4 3 2 1

Visit us at www.peterpauper.com

Be Yourself

Everyone Else Is
Already Taken

Introduction
*Be yourself—Everyone else
is already taken.*

Oscar Wilde got it right when he penned this
droll advice about being yourself. True to his
sentiment, this little handbook to audacious
living offers up insight and inspiration for
being true to your wonderful self. As Anne
Lamott writes, "We begin to find and become
ourselves when we notice how we are already
found, already truly, entirely, wildly, messily,
marvelously who we were born to be."

The thing that is really hard,
and really amazing,
is giving up on being perfect
and beginning the work
of becoming yourself.

ANNA QUINDLEN

Always be a first-rate version of yourself, instead of a second-rate version of somebody else.

JUDY GARLAND

To thine own self be true, and it must follow, as the night the day, thou canst not then be false to any man.

WILLIAM SHAKESPEARE,
Hamlet

Just as you would not neglect seeds that you planted with the hope that they will bear vegetables and fruits and flowers, so you must attend to and nourish the garden of your becoming.

JEAN HOUSTON

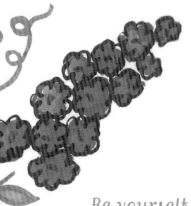

Be yourself.
Above all, let who you are,
what you are, what you believe,
shine through every sentence you
write, every piece you finish.

JOHN JAKES

He who trims himself to suit everyone will soon whittle himself away.

RAYMOND HULL

*Don't compromise
yourself. You are
all you've got.*

JANIS JOPLIN

*The most
exhausting thing
in life is being
insincere.*

ANNE MORROW LINDBERGH

Why try to be someone you're not? Life is hard enough without adding impersonation to the skills required.

ROBERT BRAULT

I have an everyday religion that works for me. Love yourself first, and everything else falls into line.

LUCILLE BALL

You shouldn't have to sacrifice who you are just because somebody else has a problem with it.

FROM "SEX AND THE CITY"
Television Show

*Being myself includes
taking risks with myself,
taking risks on new behavior,
trying new ways of
"Being Myself," so that I can
see how it is I want to be.*

HUGH PRATHER

If you must love your neighbor as yourself, it is at least as fair to love yourself as your neighbor.

NICHOLAS DE CHAMFORT

If God had wanted me otherwise, He would have created me otherwise.

JOHANN VON GOETHE

Know what
you want.
Become your
real self.

DAVID HAROLD FINK

If I am not for myself,
who will be for me?
If I am only for myself,
what am I?
And if not now, when?

RABBI HILLEL

*Be true to your
work, your word,
and your friend.*

RALPH WALDO EMERSON

A human being is only interesting
if he's in contact with himself.
I learned you have to trust yourself,
be what you are, and do what you
ought to do the way you should do it.
You have got to discover you,
what you do, and trust it.

BARBRA STREISAND

He who is in love with himself has at least this advantage— he won't encounter many rivals.

GEORG C. LICHTENBERG

It took me
a long time not
to judge myself
through someone
else's eyes.

SALLY FIELD

You can listen to what
everybody says, but the
fact remains that you've
got to get out there and
do the thing yourself.

JOAN SUTHERLAND

If you really do put a small value upon yourself, rest assured that the world will not raise your price.

AUTHOR UNKNOWN

No one can make
you feel inferior
without your
consent.

ELEANOR ROOSEVELT

Without a humble but reasonable confidence in your own powers you cannot be successful or happy.

NORMAN VINCENT PEALE

The snow goose need not bathe to make itself white. Neither need you do anything but be yourself.

LAO TZU

*If you don't run
your own life,
somebody else will.*

JOHN ATKINSON

Oliver Wendell Holmes once
attended a meeting in which he
was the shortest man present.
"Dr. Holmes," quipped a friend,
"I should think you'd feel rather
small among us big fellows."
"I do," retorted Holmes,
"I feel like a dime among a
lot of pennies."

AUTHOR UNKNOWN

You have to develop a style that suits you and pursue it, not just develop a bag of tricks. Always be yourself.

JIMMY STEWART

At bottom every man knows well enough that he is a unique being, only once on this earth; and by no extraordinary chance will such a marvelously picturesque piece of diversity in unity as he is, ever be put together a second time.

FRIEDRICH NIETZSCHE

Be who you are and say
what you feel, because
those who mind don't
matter and those who
matter don't mind.

DR. SEUSS

I was once afraid of people saying, "Who does she think she is?" Now I have the courage to stand and say, "This is who I am."

OPRAH WINFREY

You, yourself,
as much as anybody
in the entire universe,
deserve your love
and affection.

BUDDHA

*You have a masterpiece inside you,
too, you know. One unlike any that
has ever been created, or ever will be.
And remember: If you go to your grave
without painting your masterpiece,
it will not get painted. No one else
can paint it. Only you.*

GORDON MACKENZIE

*I am still learning—how to take joy
in all the people I am, how to use
all my selves in the service of what
I believe, how to accept when I fail
and rejoice when I succeed.*

AUDRE LORDE

You must have control of the authorship of your own destiny. The pen that writes your life story must be held in your own hand.

IRENE C. KASSORLA

I have a basic philosophy that I've tried to follow during my coaching career. Whether you're winning or losing, it's important to always be yourself. You can't change because of the circumstances around you.

COTTON FITZSIMMONS

*You were born
an original.
Don't die a copy.*

JOHN MASON

*If you doubt yourself,
then indeed you stand
on shaky ground.*

HENRIK IBSEN

*All the knowledge
I possess everyone else
can acquire, but my
heart is all my own.*

JOHANN VON GOETHE

Embrace your uniqueness. Time is much too short to be living someone else's life.

KOBI YAMADA

*One of the lessons that
I grew up with was to always
stay true to yourself and never
let what somebody else says
distract you from your goals.
And so when I hear about
negative and false attacks,
I really don't invest any
energy in them, because
I know who I am.*

MICHELLE OBAMA

It is better to be hated for what you are then to be loved for something you are not.

ANDRÉ GIDE

And remember, no
matter where you go,
there you are.

CONFUCIUS

Just being yourself,
being who you are,
is a successful
rebellion.

AUTHOR UNKNOWN

Take your life in your own hands, and what happens? A terrible thing: no one to blame.

ERICA JONG

Often people attempt to live their lives backwards; they try to have more things, or more money, in order to do more of what they want, so they will be happier. The way it actually works is the reverse. You must first be who you really are, then do what you need to do, in order to have what you want.

MARGARET YOUNG

*By being yourself,
you put something
wonderful in the
world that was not
there before.*

EDWIN ELLIOT

I think of life itself now as a wonderful play that I've written for myself, and so my purpose is to have the utmost fun playing my part.

SHIRLEY MACLAINE

I took a deep breath
and listened to the
old bray of my heart.
I am. I am. I am.

SYLVIA PLATH

We begin to find and become
ourselves when we notice
how we are already found,
already truly, entirely,
wildly, messily, marvelously
who we were born to be.

ANNE LAMOTT

*Never be bullied
into silence. Never
be made a victim.
Accept no one's
definition of your life;
define yourself.*

HARVEY FIERSTEIN

I find the less you
focus on your flaws,
the better off you are.
Be yourself and be glad
of who you are.

MICHELLE PFEIFFER

There is just one life for each of us: our own.

EURIPIDES

You have to leave the city of
your comfort and go into the
wilderness of your intuition.
What you'll discover
will be yourself.

ALAN ALDA

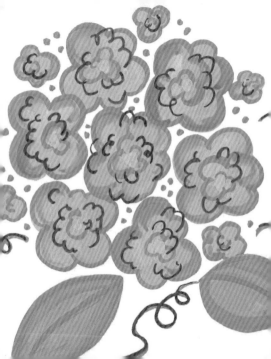

Accept everything about yourself—
I mean everything. You are you and
that is the beginning and the end—
no apologies, no regrets.

CLARK MOUSTAKAS

*Resolve to be thyself;
and know that he
who finds himself,
loses his misery.*

MATTHEW ARNOLD

The hardest battle you're ever going to fight is the battle to be just you.

LEO BUSCAGLIA

What keeps you going isn't some fine
destination but just the road you're on,
and the fact that you know how to drive.
You keep your eyes open, you see this
damned-to-hell world you got born into,
and you ask yourself, "What life can I live
that will let me breathe in and out and
love somebody or something and not run
off screaming into the woods?"

BARBARA KINGSOLVER

There is only one you for all time. Fearlessly be yourself.

AUTHOR UNKNOWN

To be one's self, and unafraid whether right or wrong, is more admirable than the easy cowardice of surrender to conformity.

IRVING WALLACE

We must always base our commitment in the center of our own being, or else no commitment will be ultimately authentic.

ROLLO MAY

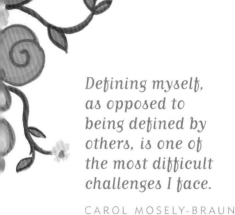

*Defining myself,
as opposed to
being defined by
others, is one of
the most difficult
challenges I face.*

CAROL MOSELY-BRAUN

It is the chiefest
point of happiness
that a man is willing
to be what he is.

DESIDERIUS ERASMUS

Knowing others is intelligence; knowing yourself is true wisdom. Mastering others is strength; mastering yourself is true power.

LAO-TZU, *Tao Te Ching*

The only person
better than you is
the person you've
yet to become.

JULIET DILLINGER